ISBN 978-0-365-64803-1
PIBN 11257590

1 MONTH OF
FREE
READING

at

www.ForgottenBooks.com

By purchasing this book you are eligible for one month membership to ForgottenBooks.com, giving you unlimited access to our entire collection of over 1,000,000 titles via our web site and mobile apps.

To claim your free month visit:

www.forgottenbooks.com/free1257590

English
Français
Deutsche
Italiano
Español
Português

www.forgottenbooks.com

Mythology Photography **Fiction**
Fishing Christianity **Art** Cooking
Essays Buddhism Freemasonry
Medicine **Biology** Music **Ancient**
Egypt Evolution Carpentry Physics
Dance Geology **Mathematics** Fitness
Shakespeare **Folklore** Yoga Marketing
Confidence Immortality Biographies
Poetry **Psychology** Witchcraft
Electronics Chemistry History **Law**
Accounting **Philosophy** Anthropology
Alchemy Drama Quantum Mechanics
Atheism Sexual Health **Ancient History**
Entrepreneurship Languages Sport
Paleontology Needlework Islam
Metaphysics Investment Archaeology
Parenting Statistics Criminology
Motivational

UNITED STATES DEPARTMENT OF AGRICULTURE
Bureau of Agricultural Economics
Division of Farm Management
and
Land Economics

-----O-------

_____

THE PROGRESS OF FARMERS IN NORTHEASTERN MONTANA

FOR TWO YEARS

-----O-----

.The farm business and financial condition of the same farmers
in Sheridan and Daniels Counties for two successive years.

-----O-----

PRELIMINARY REPORT

Washington, D. C.
December 1923

The United States Department of Agriculture and the State colleges and experiment stations of the spring and winter wheat regions, in conformity with the research program laid out for 1922, the object of which was to determine the systems of farming, the methods and practices in crop and livestock production best suited to different parts of the region, and the financial situation confronting the farmers, continued the investigation in 1923. The investigation, in addition to the area covered in this report, included other areas in Montana, North and South Dakota, Colorado, and Kansas. Further reports will be issued as the analysis of the information becomes available.

In the summer of 1922 an investigation was made among farmers of Northeastern Montana and the results were published in a report "Farming in Northeastern Montana." In 1923 a record of progress was obtained from most of the men who were interviewed the previous year. This report supersedes the previous one and shows the progress and the comparative changes in the farming and financial situation for the years 1921 and 1922. The general information given in the first report is not repeated here. However, this information is available to any who may wish to obtain it.

THE PROGRESS OF FARMERS IN

NORTHEASTERN MONTANA FOR TWO YEARS

The farm business and financial condition of farmers in Sheridan and Daniels
Counties for two successive years.

by

L. A. Reynoldson.

All things considered, the year 1922 was slightly more
favorable financially than was 1921, for farmers in Northeastern
Montana. In both years, however, good yields were obtained on
most farms. Two favorable crop years coming together as they
did were the cause for the financial progress made by many farmers and the prevalence of a spirit of optimism by some as to the
future.

With five successive years of partial or complete crop
failure from 1916 to 1920, followed by two successful crop years,
this area is a good example of the financial recovery which can be
made in a short period. Whether a further recovery is made in
1923 depends on the price that farmers get for their wheat, as
there was only a fair yield in most of the area.

Most of the farmers in 1922 placed as much dependence on
wheat for their main source of income as they did in 1921. With
our present consumption of flax exceeding the domestic supply, it
would seem that flax would be a desirable and profitable substitute for a small part of the wheat on many of the farms in this
area.

Note — It was impossible to interview every man again from
whom a report was obtained the first year. Five of the men had
abandoned their farms and left the country after harvesting and
selling their 1922 crops and some were not at home when the
enumerators visited their farms. In addition, a few reports
were discarded because of apparent inconsistencies. In no instance
were any men passed by or reports discarded because of the financial standing of the individual.

The total value of all marketable products in 1922 showed
a good increase over 1921. Even with two good crops of wheat in
succession a few farmers were forced to leave their farms because of
inability to pay the interest on the indebtedness contracted during
the preceding years of partial or total crop failure. There are
other farmers in the area who are still holding on, but who undoubtedly
will lose their farms because of over-indebtedness. As stated in
the report for 1921, the practice of carefully saving the surplus
cash from the good years to help carry over during years of failure
can not be too strongly emphasized, especially when yields of wheat
are as variable as they have been in the past.

Several of the interviewed farmers who were in a strong
financial position had purchased more land in 1922, thus indicating
that they felt sure of the future of farming in this area, while
others in an equally strong financial position desired to sell if
the opportunity presented itself.

A higher standard of living was in evidence on many farms
in 1923 than in the preceding year. This was evidenced by somewhat
greater use of produce raised on the farm, more extended use of
automobiles already owned, and new improvements made about the house.

Perhaps the best indication of a partial recovery and a
step in advancement was the fact that a majority of the men interviewed were able to reduce their accumulated indebtedness in some
degree.

There is still some abandoned crop land on the farms
visited, but the acreage was less than the previous year. Considerable idle State and non-resident-owned land formerly planted to
crops is in evidence. Under present general farming conditions,
it will be some time before this idle land is again used for growing
crops. Most of this idle land was originally farmed by men who
left the country following the several years of crop failure. The
farmers who remain are not renting this land, first, because of
the weeds and other pests with which it is infested; second, because
many are not financially able to farm an increased acreage; and third
because the present price of agricultural products is not an incentive
to greatly increased crop acreage.

Acquisition and Time of Settlement

The method of acquiring land and the time of settlement
for the 116 farmers, together with the first cost and size of the
farms on which they settled, and the value and size of their farms
at present, are given in Table 1.

Table 1 - Method of acquisition and time of settlement
of 116 farmers

| Method of acquisition | Time of settlement | | | | | | | | All | |
| | 1908 and earlier | | 1909 to 1912 | | 1913 to 1916 | | 1917 to 1920 | | | |
	Home-stead	Pur-chase	Home-stead	Pur-chase	Home-stead	Pur-chase	Home-stead	Home-chase	Home-stead	Pur-chase
No. of farmers	18	none	54	3	13	11	1	16	86	30
Average acres per farm	299	"	317	317	283	274	320	257	309	268
Average cost of land	$98	"	$99	$490	$345	$3314	$92	$3752	$136	$3265
Average value of improvements	none	"	none	$ 67	none	$ 278	none	$ 117	none	$ 171
Avg. cost of land & impts.	$ 98	"	$ 99	$557	$345	$3592	$ 92	$3869	$136	$3436
Avg. cost of land & impts, per acre	$.33	"	$.31	$1.76	$1.20	$13.10	$.29	$ 16	$.44	$12.82
Avg.acres per farm 3/1/1923	533		406		356		295		399	
Avg. value of improvements March 1, 1923	$2853		$1798		$1555		$1115		$1812	
Avg. value of land & impts. March 1, 1923	$13302		$9824		$8316		$6760		$9603	

Of the 30 men who purchased their original holdings,
6 obtained the land by relinquishment, 13 from private owners living
on the land, and 11 obtained Indian land through the Government.
The average cost of homesteads for the 13 farmers who settled from
1913 to 1916 was high because the land which a few of these men
homesteaded was occupied by squatters, and it was necessary to hire
lawyers to obtain clear titles to the land.

Since obtaining their original farms, 50 men have increased the sizes of their farms by purchase or homestead of
additional land. Table 2 shows the method of obtaining this
additional land, the average amount, and its cost.

Table 2- Method of obtaining additional land, the amount
and cost

| Method of acquisition | Year of acquiring additional land | | | | | | | | All | |
| | 1909 - 1912 | | 1913 - 1916 | | 1917 - 1920 | | 1921 - 1922 | | | |
	Home-stead	Pur-chase	Home-stead	Pur-chase	Home-stead	Pur-chase	Home-stead	Pur-chase	Home-stead	Pur-chase
No. of farmers	1	3	5	17	2	19	none	3	8	42
Avg. acres of additional land	160	160	112	282	180	265	"	320	135	284
Average cost	$50	$1766	$ 39	$4714	$36	$5249	"	$6597	$ 40	$4804
Average cost per acre	$ .31	$11.04	$.35	$16.72	$.20	$19.31	"	$21.62	$.29	$18.20

      The eight men who obtained additional land by homestead
were men who settled previous to 1909 when only 160 acres were
obtainable under the Homestead Act. When the limit was raised to
320, they, or their wives, took other homesteads. While the average
size of homestead in 1908 or earlier was 299 acres, this was due
to the fact that previous to marriage the husband and wife each took
160 acres and later combined their holdings. The purchase price of
land per acre has been increasing gradually since 1909.

Trends of Yields

      The average yields and value per acre of wheat, flax, and
oats for different years on the farms visited are given in Table 3.

Table 3 - Trend of yields and values per acre of wheat, flax, and oats

	W h e a t			F l a x			O a t s		
Year	Average yield per acre	Price per bushel*	Acre value	Average yield per acre	Price per bushel*	Acre value	Average yield per acre	Price per bushel*	Acre value
1912	22.3	$0.64	$14.27	14.0	$1.12	$15.68	47.6	$0.35	$16.66
1913	12.2	0.66	8.05	9.6	1.15	11.04	21.4	0.32	6.85
1914	11.1	0.91	10.10	9.4	1.20	11.28	27.7	0.39	10.80
1915	24.5	0.78	19.11	9.1	1.70	15.47	36.9	0.32	11.81
1916	9.2	1.61	14.81	9.1	2.48	22.57	25.3	0.47	11.89
1917	8.6	1.92	16.51	5.1	2.95	15.05	14.6	0.81	11.83
1918	8.0	1.94	15.52	2.2	3.38	7.44	16.5	0.80	13.20
1919	4.0	2.35	9.40	4.0	4.40	17.60	8.1	0.91	7.37
1920	5.7	1.28	7.30	2.2	1.75	3.85	11.6	0.51	5.92
1921	17.0	0.85	14.45	6.4	1.40	8.96	34.0	0.34	11.56
1922	16.7	0.89	14.86	6.5	1.97	12.81	30.3	0.37	11.21

*December 1, farm price per bushel for Montana from Division of
Livestock and Crop Estimates.

In five of the eleven years, the yield of wheat was below 10
bushels per acre, and it was only during these same five years that the
price of wheat was over $1.00 per bushel. It was also during this time
that costs were high. These years of low yields and not so much present
prices explain in a large measure why many farmers have failed. The acre
value of flax exceeded that for wheat in five of the eleven years, and the
returns from oats exceeded those from wheat for two years during the eleven.

Size of Farms

The number of farms of different sizes and the amount of rented
land are given in Table 4.

Table 4 - Number of farms of different sizes, 1921 and 1922

Size of farms 1921 (acres)	Number of farms	1 9 2 1 Acres			1 9 2 2 Acres		
		Operated	Owned	Rented	Operated	Owned	Rented
320 & less	45	304	296	8	313	294	19
321 - 480	29	427	334	93	432	351	81
481 - 640	23	602	381	221	594	375	219
641 & over	19	977	665	312	962	658	304
A l l	116	504	383	121	505	384	121

In 1921, 54 men rented some land in addition to what they owned and 55 rented some in 1922. Four men in 1921 rented out some land and 5 rented out some in 1922.

Crops

The acreages of the different crops in 1921 and 1922 on farms with different numbers of crop-acres are shown in Table 5.

Table 5 - Average number of acres of different crops

No. of acres in crops 1921	Number of farms	Average acres in crops	Wheat acres	Oats for grain acres	Flax acres	Corn acres	Oats for hay acres	Other hay acres	Other crops acres
				1921 crops					
Less than 100	7	66	49	5	8	--	1	3	--
100 - 199	51	153n	112	19	5	4	8	4	1
200 - 299	31	232	162	25	9	5	12	8	11
300 and over	27	426	317	55	10	14	8	10	12
All	116	232	169	28	7	6	9	7	6
				1922 crops					
Less than 100	7	109	72	10	21	1	4	1	--
100 - 199	51	177	132	17	7	4	10	4	3
200 - 299	31	234	167	21	6	6	15	4	15
300 and over	27	441	325	36	12	9	17	9	33
All	116	250	182	22	9	6	13	5	13

The area in crops was 8 per cent greater in 1922 than in 1921. Much of the increase in crop acreage was at the expense of summer fallow. In 1921, there was an average of 37 acres of summer fallow per farm and in 1922 only 26 acres. Likewise, the number of men who had fallow land decreased from 66 to 45. Some of these men were hoping to recoup a part of their past losses through increased crop acreages, but if the crop has been a failure more of them would have been forced to abandon their farms.

Even though efforts were made by different agencies to have farmers reduce their wheat acreage in 1922, the effect was not apparent in this area. In both years wheat occupied 73 per cent of the crop acreage on the farms visited. Thus nearly three-fourths of the increase in crop area which averaged 18 acres per farm was planted to wheat. For the other crops there was no important change.

Until more livestock is produced on these farms, there perhaps will be no great variation from the present corn acreage. The average yield of fodder in 1921 was two and one-half tons and in 1922 it was two tons. Very little corn was husked.

Livestock

The livestock on these farms was essentially the same for both years. On March 1, 1923, the average number and value of the different kinds of livestock were as follows:

```
 8 work horses per farm valued at $75.00 per head
 2 other   "    "    "    "    "    55.00  "    "
 5 milk cows   "    "    "    "    49.00  "    "
 1 range cow   "    "    "    "    34.00  "    "
 7 other cattle "   "    "    "    27.00  "    "
 2 hogs        "    "    "    "    21.00  "    "
.44 head of poultry per farm"    "     .61  "    "
```

Any material change in the number of livestock would be noticeable only over a longer term of years. There is, however, an opportunity to increase the number of cattle on farms, especially range cattle, as there is a large amount of idle land, both State and privately owned, which could be used for grazing. Increasing the number of cattle would also tend to increase the corn acreage. More of the fallow land could be planted to corn if there was stock to eat the crop and the large amount of labor now expended on cultivating this fallow land would then produce a valuable feed crop.

Production for Market

The principal products sold during both years, or for sale at the end of the year, are shown in Table 6. Other products, such as milk, dressed meats, and poultry, were sold, but the total value of each is considerably less than for any of those given.

Table 6 - Principal farm products sold or held for sale

Product	No. of farmers 1921	Total amount 1921	Average price 1921	Total value 1921	No. of farmers 1922	Total amount 1922	Average price 1922	Total value 1922
Hard wheat	83	185,021 bu.*	$1.10	$203,676	106	266,441 bu.*	$ .99	$262,905
Soft wheat	67	97,221 " *	.70	68,088	51	59,016 " *	.76	44,628
Flax	26	3,576 " *	1.73	6,170	28	5,193 " *	2.12	10,986
Oats	27	9,277 " *	.40	3,677	18	8,080 " *	.40	3,194
Cows	12	36	38.00	1,384	30	120	39.00	4,659
Calves	17	44	22.00	976	26	96	18.00	1,684
Steers	16	43	43.00	1,859	41	119	45.00	5,375
Hogs	12	30	24.00	698	9	36	21.00	765
Pigs	18	107	5.00	505	25	253	11.00	2,854
Butter	57	18,891 lbs.	.27	5,135	61	19,536 lbs.	.27	5,200
Butterfat	40	10,499 "	.24	2,553	39	9,564 "	.25	2,359
Eggs	70	13,769 doz.	.21	2,838	69	12,959 doz.	.21	2,744

*The figures for wheat, flax, and oats show the total bushels of such
grain for sale in both years. This grain was not all sold the
year it was grown, but a part held over and sold the following year.
However, the total amount of grain raised for sale is used in com-
puting the volume of the year's cash business.

The table shows the great importance of wheat as a source of cash
income. Sale of the 1921 and 1922 wheat crops made up 84 per cent and 81
per cent of the total value of the commodities produced for sale in these
years.

The total value of the principal products was approximately $429 per
farm greater in 1922 than for 1921. The sales value of crops per farm for 1921
and 1922 averaged $2486 and $2835 respectively; of livestock, $64 and $144, and
livestock products, $108 and $97.

In 1921, butter ranked third in importance in the total
value of sales, while in 1922 steers which in 1921 were seventh in importance,
came up to third place. If more dependence were placed each year on these
and similar products, more farms would be on a self-sustaining basis irrespective
of wheat yields and prices.

Family Living from the Farm

The total amount of the commodities produced at home (butter, milk,
eggs, meat, and garden) used by the family increased somewhat in 1922.

House rent was the largest single item of family living contributed by the farm in 1922; the average amount credited was $121 per farm.

The value of milk, butter, and eggs used by the family averaged $115 per farm; meat (beef, pork, and poultry) averaged $72, while garden products (including potatoes) amounted to only $41 per farm. The fine gardens seen on some of the farms and the quantity of vegetables and small fruits obtained from them indicate that on most of the farms more time could be devoted profitably to providing a good garden for the family.

Outside Earnings

It is interesting to note what means of earning more money some of these farmers have employed to supplement their earnings from farming activities. Table 7 shows the outside earnings, the size of farm, and crop acres.

Table 7 - Outside earnings of farmers, size of farm, and crop
acres by time of settlement

		Date of settling				
		1908 and earlier	1909-1912	1913-1916	1917-1920	All farms
Number of farmers		18	57	24	17	116
Outside earnings	1921	$40	$ 46	$ 65	$ 163	$ 66
	1922	45	71	89	278	101
Size of farm	1921	623	481	518	435	504
	1922	618	496.	501	422	505
Crop acres	1921	335	225	208	183	232
	1922	334	340	244	195	250

The average outside earnings for both years for all groups increased as length of residence decreased. In 1922 the earnings for each group were larger than they were for 1921. The difference in the number of crop acres might seem altogether responsible for the earnings of the men who settled in different periods, as those who had the smallest crop acreage would have more time to do outside work. This, however, is not the reason, as some men have from force of necessity turned to outside work as an aid in supporting themselves and their families. Harvesting, working on threshing crews, and hauling grain are some of the ways by which the farm income is supplemented.

Cash Receipts and Expenses

Actual and available cash is the item of greatest importance to farmers of this area. Table 6 shows that wheat is the product from which the bulk of the cash receipts were derived both years. In 1921 the returns were $2,343 and in 1922 they were $2,651. The "actual cash receipts" do not always tell the entire story as many farmers have not sold all their grain by the first of March, especially those who belong to cooperative wheat marketing associations. Table 10 shows that on March 1, 1923 the average value of crops on hand was considerably in excess of the previous year. These crops, if sold during the year, would add considerably to the cash receipts of that year.

The total average cash receipts for the 116 farmers in 1921 amounted to $2,801 and in 1922 to $3,269, an increase of $468, or about 17 per cent.

The largest single item of expense each year was usually for threshing. In 1921, this item averaged $332 and in 1922, $353 per farm. The second large item of expense was for hired labor. In 1921, there were 72 men who hired some labor, the average cost of which was $189. In 1922 there were 91 men who hired labor at an average cost of $204. The increase in the total cost of labor was not due to an increased day rate, but to labor being hired for a longer period because of a better crop year in 1922. This expense of hired labor does not include that of threshing labor, which is included in the cost of threshing.

The total average cash expenses were $2,010 in 1921 and $1,932 in 1922. The item of cash expense does not include the amount spent for family living or for the reduction of indebtedness. The amount of the difference between cash receipts and expenses has to provide for family living, reduction of debts, and any savings that can be made.

Farm Income*

Farm incomes in 1921 and 1922 from farms with different numbers of crop acres are shown in Table 8.

---

*Farm Income, as given here, does not include the value of products raised on the farm and used by the family.

Table 8 - Relation of farm income to acres in crops

Crop acres 1921	Number of farmers	1921		1922	
		Average acres in crops	Average farm income	Average acres in crops	Average farm income
Less than 100	7	66	$ 380	109	$ 796
100 - 199	51	153	811	177	1,102
200 - 299	31	232	1,355	235	1,164
300 and over	27	426	2,039	441	2,439
A l l	116	232	$1,217	250	$1,411

For the 116 farmers in 1922, there was an average increase
of $194 in the average farm income over that of the preceding year. The
number of crop acres for both years had considerable bearing on the total
amount of the farm income, for as the average number of crop acres increased, likewise did the average farm income. However, there is no
relationship between number of crop acres and farm income per acre, as
the men with the smaller numbers of crop acres add more to their farm
incomes from outside earnings than do those with a larger number of acres
in crops.

The number of farmers with farm incomes of different amounts for
1921 and the farm incomes of 1922 for the same men are shown in Table 9.

Table 9 - Number of farmers with farm incomes of different sizes
in 1922 compared with their 1921 incomes

1921		1922						
Farm income	Number of farmers	Farm expenses greater than receipts	0 to $999	$1000 to $1999	$2000 to $2999	$3000 and over	Number of farmers	Average farm income
		No.	No.	No.	No.	No.		
Farm expenses greater than receipts	13	2	6	4	1	--	13	$ 666
0 - $ 999	47	7	23	13	3	1	47	856
$1000 - 1999	32	5	7	12	6	2	32	1306
2000 - 2999	17	1	3	5	5	3	17	2114
3000 & over	7	--	--	1	2	4	7	5284
A l l	116	15	39	35	17	10	116	$1411

Eleven of the 13 men who in 1921 had farm expenses in excess of farm
receipts were able to reverse their position in 1922. Thirteen men who had
receipts in excess of expenses in 1921 has expenses in excess of receipts in
1922.

Assets

The average value of both real and personal property on March 1, 1922 and 1923 is shown in Table 10.

Table 10 - Value of real estate, equipment and other miscellaneous items
(Average for all farms)

Items	March 1, 1922	March 1, 1923
Real estate	$9,363	$9,603
Livestock	1,251	1,285
Machinery	763	661
Automobiles	150	130
Engines and separators	228	220
Feed and supplies	550	439
Crops on hand	325	469
Other assets	331	473
Household goods	182	193

The average increase in value of real estate was due to the purchase of some land and to the increased valuation placed on their land by a few men. The average estimated value per acre of land increased from $24 to $25. Very little change took place in the value of dwellings, other buildings, fences, livestock, engines, and separators, and household goods. The decrease in the value of machinery of over $100 for the year was due chiefly to depreciation of old machines combined with comparatively few purchases of new machinery. The decrease in value of automobiles was all due to depreciation. More grain was on hand March 1, 1923, than the previous year because many of the men interviewed had joined a wheat pool during the year; consequently a larger amount of grain was being held. "Other assets" principally cash on hand or debts due increased from $331 to $473.

The number of tractors and engines owned by the 116 men increased during the two years from 29 to 32 and the number of grain separators increased from 8 to 14. Automobiles and trucks were owned on 76 farms in 1921 and on 80 farms in 1922, but because of high running expense some machines had not been operated in either of the years.

Indebtedness

The amount of the indebtedness which different numbers of farmers were carrying on March 1, 1923, was as follows:

        22 men had no indebtedness;
        18 men had indebtedness of less than $2,000;
        37 men had indebtedness of $2,000 to $3,999;
        24 men had indebtedness of 4,000 to 5,999;
         7 men had indebtedness of 6,000 to 7,999;
    and 8 men had indebtedness of 8,000 ot more.

The average indebtedness of the 116 men on March 1, 1922, was $3,522, and on March 1, 1923, it was $3,156, a decrease of $366.

Table 11 shows the kind, number, and amount of the principal liabilities which these man had The bulk of indebtedness is secured by mortgages, most of which draw high rates of interest. The first year of the sruvey very few Federal farm loans were found. However, during the past year a number of these men were able to substitute Federal farm loans for their ordinary first mortgages. This in itself is a great help as the amount of interest is lower and the principal is rediced seni-annually.

Table 11 - Number and amounts of mortgages and other debts

Form of liability	March 1, 1922		March 1, 1923	
	Number of farmers	Average amount	Number of farmers	Average amount
First mortgage	92	$2,404	83	$2,437
Second "	27	1,926	27	1,882
Third. "	5	982	5	1,102
Chattel "	48	1,250	46	1,006
Back taxes	41	291	36	387
Other debts	70	847	51	687

The most significant change to be noted, as shown in this table, is the number of men who reduced their "other debts."

The progress these men have made in liquidating their indebtedness is shown in Table 12.

Table 12 - Indebtedness and liquidation of indebtedness of 116
farmers from March 1, 1922 to March 1, 1923

	Number of acres in crops 1921														
	Less than 100			100 - 199			200 - 299			300 and over			All		
No. of farms	7			51			31			27			116		
Avg.crop acres 1921	66			153			232			426			232		
Avg.crop acres 1922	109			177			235			441			250		
	No.	Amt.debt 1922 ($)	1923 ($)	No.	Amt.debt 1922 ($)	1923 ($)	No.	Amt.debt 1922 ($)	1923 ($)	No.	Amt.debt 1922 ($)	1923 ($)	No.	Amt.debt 1922 ($)	1923 ($)
Farmers with no indebtedness 1922	--	--	--	5	--	--	4	--	--	3	--	--	12	--	--
Farmers who paid off all indebtedness during year	--	--	--	2	456	--	4	1325	--	4	2756	--	10	1724	--
Farmers who reduced indebtedness during year	4	3440	3129	26	3419	2821	14	4844	4462	14	6833	5731	58	4589	3941
Farmers with no change in indebtedness during year	--	--	--	6	2200	2200	3	3133	3133	3	5527	5527	12	3265	3265
Farmers who increased indebtedness	3	2758	2912	12	3529	4041	6	3304	3847	3	5500	5682	24	3623	4057

Ten per cent of the men had no indebtedness at the beginning or the end
of the year. Of the men who had some indebtedness on March 1, 1922, 65 per cent
were able to reduce the amount during the year. The average reduction in indebtedness amounted to nearly 20 per cent of their total liabilities.

Nearly 15 per cent of the men paid off all their obligations so that on
March 1, 1923, there were 19 per cent of all the men who had no debts.

Those men who did not change the amount of their liabilities were able to pay their taxes, interest, and other expenses. There was an increase of about 12 per cent in the indebtedness of 24 men during the year. Some of the increase in indebtedness was due entirely to unpaid taxes or interest. A number of the men who further increased their liabilities during the year will eventually lose their farms and be forced to quit. These are not necessarily the men with the largest liabilities.

The net worth of the 116 farmers on March 1, 1922 and the gain or loss they made the following year are shown in Table 1e.

Table 13 - Net worth of 116 farmers, on March 1, 1922, and the gain or loss made the following year

Net worth March 1 1922	Number of farmers	Loss, 1922			Gain, 1922				
		$2000 and over	$1000 to -1999	0 to $999	$1 to $999	$1000 to 1999	$2000 to 2999	$3000 to 3999	$4000 and over
$-2000 to 3999	1			1					
$-1 to $-1999	2			2					
Less than $2000	8			1	2	1	3	1	
$2000 to 3999	14			3	8	1	2		
4000 to 5999	16			7	3	4	2		
6000 to 7999	14		1	3	7	2	1		
8000 to 9999	18			7	7	4			
10000 to 11999	12		1	2	4	2		1	2
12000 to 13999	15	1	1	5	4	4			
14000 and over	16	1	1	1	4	4	3	1	1
All	116	2	4	32	39	32	11	3	3

Even with a good crop year in 1922, nearly 33 per cent of the men showed a loss in new worth for the year. However, the average net worth for the 116 farmers showed a gain. The three men in 1921 who had a minus net wroth went still further behind in 1922.

Table 14 shows the net worth of farmers in 1921 and 1922 on farms with different numbers of crop acres.

Table 14 - Net worth of farmers on farms with different numbers of
acres in crops

Crop acres in 1921	Number of farmers	1921		1922	
		Average acres in crops	Average net worth	Average acres in crops	Average net worth
Less than 100	7	66	$ 3,558	109	$ 4,290
100 - 199	51	153	7,348	177	8,064
200 - 299	31	238	9,655	235	9,942
300 and over	27	426	15,340	441	16,564
A l l	116	232	$ 9,509	250	$10,316

The average net worth of these farmers increased nearly
8 per cent during the year.

The change in net worth of farmers due to farming activities
and the change in the value of land since coming to this area are
shown in Table 15. Any increases in net worth due to outside invest-
ments and outside earnings of these men are not included in these figures.

Table 15 - Change in net worth of farmers due to farming activity and
change in value of land

		Date of settling				All farms
		1908 and earlier	1909-1912	1913-1916	1917-1920	
Number of farmers		18	57	24	17	116
Average change due to farming activities	From date of settlement to March 1, 1922	$ 9,243	$ 713	$ -87	$ -321	$ 1,720
	From March 1,1922 to March 1,1923	-44	832	965	478	671
	Total to March 1, 1923	$ 9,199	$1,545	$ 878	$ 157	$ 2,391
Average change due to change in land value	From date of settlement to March 1, 1922	$ 6,619	$6,651	$3,701	$1,222	$ 5,240
	From March 1,1922 to March 1, 1923	-78	55	156	29	52
	Total to March 1, 1922	$ 6,541	$6,706	$3,857	$1,251	$ 5,292
Average change due to farming activities and change in land values	From date of settlement to March 11, 1922	$15,862	$7,364	$3,614	$ 901	$ 6,960
	From March 1,1922 to March 1, 1923	-122	887	1,121	507	723
	Total to March 1, 1923	$15,740	$8,251	$4,735	$1,408	$ 7,683

On the average the net worth of the oldest settlers decreased slightly in 1922. This was due in a large measure to lowering of inventories of feed and supplies during the year and to a lower estimated valuation on the land.

The value placed on the farms by their owners for 1921 was considerably greater than the original cost. For 1922 some of the men felt that with two good crops and the prospect of a third good crop in 1923 their land was worth still more. Consequently the average valuation increased slightly. The average change in net worth for the year due to farming activities and change in land value was $723.

From the time they came to northeastern Montana to March 1, 1922, 91 per cent of the men had bettered themselves through their farming activities, and on March 1, 1923, this number was increased to 94 per cent.

CPSIA information can be obtained
at www.ICGtesting.com
Printed in the USA
LVHW081447211118
597922LV00010B/615/P